MUCHA

DISCOVERING ART

The Life, Times and Work of the World's Greatest Artists

MUCHA

O.B. DUANE

BROCKHAMPTON PRESS

For Cillian, Dylan and Billie, the 'almighty Trinity',
who never failed me in their encouragement.

The author wishes to acknowledge Jiri Mucha's biography of his father,
Alphonse Maria Mucha, as an invaluable source of information and inspiration for this book.

First published in Great Britain by Brockhampton Press,
an imprint of The Caxton Publishing Group,
20 Bloomsbury Street, London WC1B 3JH

ISBN 1 84186 100 6

Produced by Flame Tree Publishing,
The Long House, Antrobus Road, Chiswick, London W4 5HY
for Brockhampton Press
A Wells/McCreeth/Sullivan Production

Pictures printed courtesy of the Visual Arts Library, London,
and Edimedia, Paris.

Printed and bound by Oriental Press, Dubai

CONTENTS

Maude Adams as Joan of Arc, 1909
(Metropolitan Museum, New York).

FOREWORD

*A*rt nouveau experienced its short, sharp burst of life towards the end of the last century, roughly between 1895 and 1904, after which it relinquished itself to a newer, more refined style of art. Its influence, however, lasted far beyond its actual life.

In the 1890s, many young artists began to react to a general loss of individuality which manifested itself in art, in the adherence to academic classicism, and in society, in the spread of industrialization throughout western Europe. *Art nouveau* attempted to achieve a co-existence between functional surroundings and the intimacy of private life. It was characterized by a renewed interest in natural, flowing forms and a subjective feeling for spiritual content. Curves, spirals and rich ornamentation became popular features of the style and were applied to glass, ceramics, architecture and graphic art. The movement attempted to introduce a more soulful art to the public by exploiting new printing techniques and lithography to achieve wide circulation and low prices. After only ten years *art nouveau* was hounded out of existence and replaced by a campaign to introduce new, simple architecture, free of ornamentation, yet purposeful and enduring.

Mucha never considered himself a member of the *art nouveau* school, although he became fiercely entangled with the movement through no fault of his own. In Paris, graphic art in the *art nouveau* style became tremendously popular and posters, in particular, acquired the status of precious paintings desperately sought after by collectors. Mucha's main strengths lay in his skill as a draughtsman and in his ability to glorify natural, feminine beauty through a unique graphic fluency. He had a long, successful career spanning sixty creative years. He has left us an unparalleled collection of diverse works, not all of it in the *art nouveau* style, from posters to *panneaux*, from sculpture to spectacular historical canvases.

Gismonda, **1895** (Private collection). Printed by Lemercier, this poster is the first example of Mucha's unique graphic talent, put to use in an entirely unfamiliar field. Note the early evidence of features he went on to develop – the liberal use of ornamentation in the upper background, the arabesques and repeated circular motifs.

La Dame aux Camelias, 1896 (Private collection) is one of Mucha's best known posters and many consider it his finest. The harmonious use of colours is a particularly outstanding feature of this work.

CHAPTER 1

The Early Years

Mucha was born in July 1860 in the small South Moravian town of Ivancice. At the time of his birth, Czechoslovakia was part of the Austro-Hungarian Empire, struggling hard against the Habsburg policy of Germanization to maintain its own identity, language and customs.

Overleaf and above:
Daydream/Reverie (Private collection)
– produced by Mucha in 1896 as a single
panneau.

Opposite:
Bières de la Meuse, c. 1897 (Private
collection). One of many posters Mucha
produced while under contract to the
publisher, Champenois.

lphonse Maria Mucha's father, Andreas, was descended from a long line of Czech vine-growers. Following his release from the Imperial army, he made the decision not to preserve the family tradition, but to follow instead a more lucrative career as a court usher. Alphonse was born to Andreas' second wife, Amalie Mala, in the little stone building next to the district court. Mucha's mother, a well-educated woman, had worked as a governess for an aristocratic family in Vienna. She was quick to encourage her infant son's talent for drawing. Even as a baby, Alphonse loved to hold a pencil and she would hang one on a ribbon around his neck so that he could draw as he crawled along. When his mother took him shopping with her, he would amaze everyone around him by sitting on the floor with crayon and paper, accurately sketching the faces of the locals. Her young son had a remarkable gift for singing, too. At the age of ten, his outstanding alto voice earned him a choral scholarship at St Peter's Church, Brno. The scholarship award greatly pleased Mucha's father, as it meant that Alphonse could now also afford to attend grammar school. The early association with the church was to have a potent influence on Mucha's life and on his art. He considered church architecture to be the pinnacle of beauty and in later years decorated his studio like a church, filling his rooms with incense, religious artefacts, rich red tapestries and ecclesiastical garments.

At the age of fifteen, when his voice no longer served the needs of the choral master, Mucha was forced to abandon the choir and, with it, the relative material comforts his scholarship had afforded him. He was obliged to find accommodation elsewhere and very happily accepted a friend's offer to stay with his family in the neighbouring town of Usti-Nad-Orlici. It was here, one afternoon, that Mucha became convinced of his vocation. Julek, his young companion, took Alphonse into the local church where a painter Johann Umlaur was busy at work. Umlaur, who enjoyed a sound reputation as an artist of the old Baroque style, had been commissioned to decorate the church according to Baroque tradition. The paintings Mucha now saw before him made a deep and lasting impression. He had never before considered the artist in a current setting. He had only thought about great old masters of the past and had never properly appreciated art and painting as a living, contemporary accomplishment. He had not lost his enthusiasm for drawing throughout his childhood years, but now, finally, art presented a serious path forward. Before the end of his stay in Usti-Nad-Orlici, Mucha had made his decision to devote the rest of his life to painting.

Although his father did his utmost to convince Alphonse that an artist's life was not for him, Andreas was eventually forced to surrender to his son's ambition. He did not do this without a battle, however. Andreas secretly entertained the wish that his son Alphonse would

one day enter the priesthood. Upon Mucha's return from Usti, his father was determined to secure for him a reputable career in the eyes of the Ivancice community. He announced that he had found him a position as clerk at the court in the town. Alphonse was deeply discontented; he loathed the idea of becoming a court scribe, caged in a small room for the remainder of his days, but because no other employment was on offer, he had to take up the position. He spent all of his spare time on any activity vaguely associated with drawing. The small town of Ivancice had many social clubs, all of them in need of someone who might volunteer to paint a poster, decorate a town hall, or design an invitation to some formal community event. Mucha soon offered his services, organizing committees and clubs, painting scenery for the local amateur dramatic theatre, directing their productions, and generally giving artistic advice.

The situation in his home town did not satisfy him for long, however. Life in Ivancice was still very old-fashioned and Mucha was keen to progress and to dedicate himself to the serious study of art. It was eventually decided between his parents that he should perhaps apply to the Art Academy at Prague. Having submitted his drawings, he was received rather unenthusiastically by Professor Lhota, who recommended that Mucha abandon any idea of being an artist. 'Young man,' he said, 'there are many painters but little money. I'd advise you to find yourself another profession where you can get on better.' Mucha was disappointed with this response, but refused to give up entirely. In 1881, at the age of twenty-one, he spotted an advertisement in a Viennese newspaper which held his attention – Messrs Kautsky-Brioschi-Burghardt, makers of theatrical scenery in Vienna, required an apprentice to join them at their workshop. Mucha immediately sent off some examples of his drawings and received, in due course, a favourable response, inviting him to join the firm. There was now no reason to stay in Ivancice; he had been accepted by a firm which produced scenery for several of the leading theatres in Austria. He packed his trunks, said goodbye to his family and headed for Vienna, full of hope for the future.

Mucha was employed by Kautsky-Brioschi-Burghardt for a period of two years. He very much enjoyed the work and he took full advantage of his surroundings, visiting the theatre, art galleries and the city's old churches. His new position provided him with a good, basic knowledge of theatre and he managed, at the same time, to afford evening art classes during his stay in Vienna. He came to admire the decorative and historical painting of Hans Makart. Makart was one of the most popular artists of the day, a man who exalted the beauty of Vienna's women, not as mythological figures, but as he honestly saw them in the streets. Makart's influence prevailed, not only in painting, but in fashion and in interior design. He died suddenly at the peak of

Cycles Perfecta, *c.* 1897 (Private collection). Another example of the commercial graphic work Mucha delivered at the height of his Parisian fame.

IMP. F. CHAMPENOIS, PARIS

his popularity in 1884, but the decorative mannerisms which he applied to the female form had a forceful impact on the young Mucha, eventually weaving their way into his early work.

Mucha's time in Vienna came to an abrupt end in December 1881, when a raging fire engulfed the Ring Theatre, one of the city's largest theatrical centres and one of his employer's best customers. The firm of Kautsky-Brioschi had little option but to dismiss their most recently arrived member of staff. Mucha, however, was unperturbed. He had a superstitious belief in fate which stayed with him throughout his lifetime. He promptly left Vienna with very little money and without any particular direction or purpose in mind. Entrusting himself to fate, he made a journey by train as far as his purse would carry him, to the town of Milulov, just over the Moravian border. Mucha eventually supported himself here by painting and drawing portraits of the town's colourful inhabitants. On arrival, the young artist checked into the cheapest hotel and managed to persuade the local bookseller to hang his sketches in his shop window. Mucha had soon sketched the figure of a local lady, who was, unknown to him, the doctor's wife. The portrait was displayed in the bookseller's window, accompanied by the slogan: 'For five Florins at the Lion Hotel'. The picture and its caption unleashed a tremendous scandal in the village. Mucha had great difficulty explaining himself but, with the passing of time, he succeeded in becoming an integral part of the town's society, painting portraits, designing scenery, attending dinner parties and generally rendering himself indispensable to the community.

Fate now grasped him firmly by the hand. One of his sketches was spotted by Count Karl Khuen's estate manager and he was offered the opportunity to restore some family portraits and to decorate the newly built dining room walls of the Count's castle. Count Karl was delighted with the frescoes Mucha painted for him and was determined to hold on to his new protégé. He dissuaded Alphonse from returning to Vienna and sent him instead on a similar mission, to decorate his brother's castle at Gandegg, in the Tyrol. This was to be one of the most fulfilling times of Mucha's life. Count Egon was a keen amateur painter and he loved to visit the cultural centres of Europe. Mucha travelled with him to Milan and to Venice, all the time widening his knowledge of art. The Count had newly made the acquaintance of an art professor at the Munich Academy and he invited the professor one day to take a look at Mucha's work. It was immediately decided between the two men that the young artist had talent which ought to be properly explored and developed. Count Karl readily agreed to send Mucha to Munich at his own expense and Alphonse enrolled at the Academy in 1885 to begin his first course of academic studies.

The Munich Academy adhered to historic artistic traditions. Mucha was taught by Professors Lofftz and Herterich, both of them skilled teachers, yet old-fashioned in their ways. French art and progressive styles were unpopular at the Academy; the curriculum favoured classicism and the copying of old models. In Munich, Mucha practised his line-drawing strictly within the academic tradition. He acquired the technical polish essential for an illustrative artist, but his work of this period bears very little resemblance to the art which was to follow.

Count Karl was insistent that Mucha take his art studies a stage further. In Paris, a new age was taking shape; the city had evolved as the European centre of artistic and literary activity. It seemed the obvious place for a young artist to mature. In 1887, Mucha journeyed to Paris to enrol in the Académie Julian. He could not avoid confronting the latest theories and art movements, but refused to be drawn into theoretical disputes. Although some art students were still paying homage to Impressionist ideals, many were earnestly searching for something new. Mucha considered the new ideas insubstantial and could not support the notion of art being an end in itself. He did not wish to waste time arguing about colour and a disintegrous approach to painting. He was disinterested in whims of fashion and focused his talent on producing simple, clear, closely integrated pictures. His opinions on art always remained unambiguous and consistent: 'I do not want to be an artist if it should mean creating art for art's sake. The conception of modern art as subject to passing fashion is an insult to art.'

A year later, Mucha returned to Paris for another course of study. This time he enrolled at the Académie Colarossi and studied there from morning until evening, improving his skill and building on his reputation as a talented draughtsman. He was now twenty-eight years old and still being supported by Count Karl. In January 1889, however, Mucha received a letter from Count Karl's secretary. It contained the shocking news that the Count had decided to withdraw his allowance, that he no longer wished to act as Mucha's patron. Mucha was devastated. The abrupt termination of funds at this most crucial learning period was a source of great distress and bewilderment. He could not recall having offended the Count in any way. They had become close friends and the Count's castle, Emmahof, had become a second home for Mucha. A letter from the Count, written in 1891, sheds some light on his motive for such drastic action:

The description of your life I found very interesting; it pleased me and reassured me and, above all, I am glad about your successful struggle. The medicine was strong but good; it was only with regret that I used it, but I think the moment was correctly chosen, and I am filled with pride that it has brought results.

It is possible that Count Karl believed his continued financial patronage would leave Mucha ill-prepared for the realities of life.

Opposite, above and overleaf:
The Four Seasons/Les Saisons was the first collection of *panneaux* commissioned by Mucha's new publisher, Champenois. The *panneaux* were a huge commercial success and made their way into the homes of many Parisians in 1896 (Private collection).

Perhaps he had grown to acknowledge and approve of a relationship between art and suffering. Whatever the Count's reason for withdrawing his money, it came as a complete surprise to Mucha, who now found himself in a grave dilemma. He could not finish his studies at the Académie Colarossi. He was utterly penniless and knew that Paris was not a city which readily tolerated poverty. For the first time in his adult life, he was forced to stand on his own two feet and to devise a way of earning a living by means of his art. Mucha's departure from the Académie was followed by two years of terrible deprivation. He had experienced poverty as a boy when his scholarship had come to an end, but Paris was an expensive city, demanding that the successful artist socialize. Mucha was forced to retreat, he would rather have suffered hunger or exposure than borrow from anybody. He restricted himself to a diet of boiled lentils which he cooked in an old tin pot over the fire.

Mucha spent many wretched months, freezing and exhausted in his tiny room in the rue Bara. He searched for whatever work he could possibly find. He was fairly well-known in parts of the city as a reliable, honest, hard-working illustrator and he did manage to secure some commissions. He drew cut-out soldiers for children's books for the publisher Levy, he drew illustrations for less fashionable journals and periodicals, such as *Le Petit Francais Illustré*, he also sent some drawings back to Prague in the hope of getting work. At this time, he was visited by Monsieur Henri Bourrelier, an enthusiastic young man who worked for the publisher Armand Colin and was always on the look out for fresh talent. Bourrelier played an important part in reviving Mucha's spirits. Hearing of Mucha's circumstances, Bourrelier called on him at rue Bara. He abruptly sent for the doctor, commissioned some illustrations, gave Mucha an advance on the drawings and helped get him back into circulation. An old Polish friend named Slewinski, who had studied with Mucha at the Académie Colarossi, also helped him at this time. He encouraged his unhappy friend to move from his shabby accommodation to a more acceptable room in rue de la Grande Chaumière. The hostel, located directly opposite the Académie Colarossi, was owned by Madame Charlotte and was a popular hive of student activity. Madame Charlotte played hostess to a wide range of artistic types, painters, playwrights, poets, actors, all of different nationality, each of them struggling to express their own individual philosophy of life and make a name for themselves in Paris.

Mucha's first firm recognition as an artist came when the publisher Jouvet requested that he illustrate a book of fairy tales, *Les Contes des Grand-mères*, by Xavier Marmier. Some of the drawings were subsequently exhibited at the Salon, which brought public acclaim for the first time and a very favourable critics' response. To exhibit at the Salon was beyond his wildest dreams and it helped dramatically to boost his self-confidence.

Salon des Cent, 1896 (Private collection). Mucha designed this poster for an exhibition at the gallery belonging to the prestigious *La Plume* magazine, unaware at the time that he would soon have his own exhibition there.

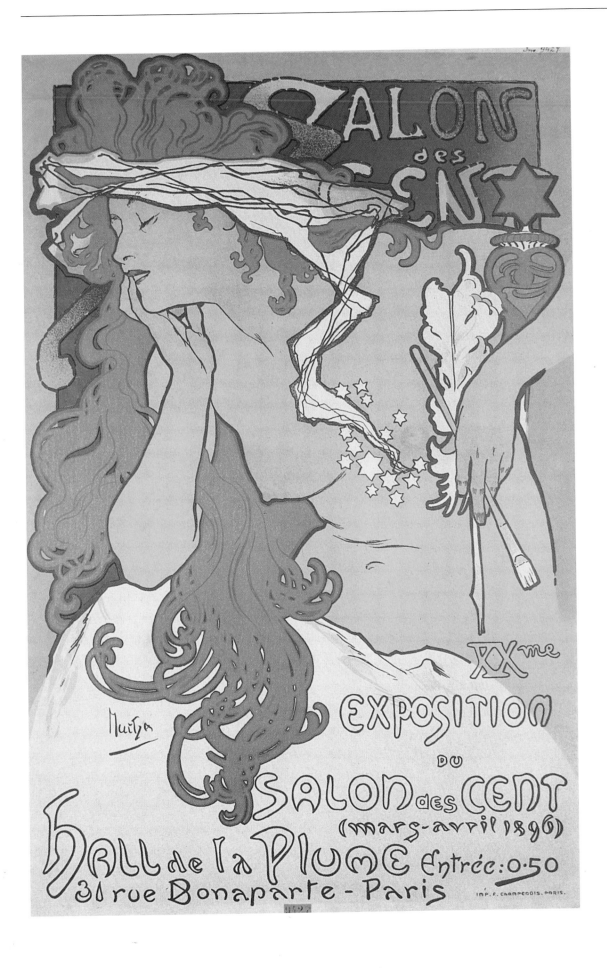

Yet more work followed. The drawings he had sent to Prague met with admiration and approval and Mucha was asked to illustrate an epic poem entitled *The Adamites,* written by the Czech poet, Svatopluk. The story of this epic had an immediate appeal. He had been brought up in a climate of nationalist fervour and had strong patriotic feelings. Everywhere he went, he made friends with Slavic people; he organized societies, such as the Slav circle *Lada,* and he became President of the Czech society *Beseda. The Adamites* described the life and annihilation of the religious sect that was part of the Hussite movement. Mucha wanted to turn this project into something far more elaborate. He would have liked to have painted these episodes of Czech history on large canvases. Practical concerns prevented him from fulfilling this ambition. He drew everything at this time for money, employing his craftsmanship as he had learned it under the guidance of his Munich professors. He still lived economically and was struggling to survive. He sketched the drawings for the publisher in the academic style instilled in him at the Munich Academy, displaying a remarkable graphic fluency, coupled with an instinctive feeling for composition, but his art at this juncture did not deviate from contemporary expectation and was not particularly original. The work he was now undertaking however, became increasingly prestigious. He began to illustrate for more well-known magazines including *La Vie Parisienne, Le Monde Illustré* and *Le Figaro Illustré.* He also completed many projects for the publication *Le Costume au Théâtre.* He was perfectly well able to capture facial expressions, the contour lines of the female form, the sensuous folds in the drapery. He re-acquainted himself with the theatre, sketching costumes and stage sets and meeting new theatrical friends. He never liked to work without a model. When he could not afford to employ one, as was frequently the case, he photo-graphed or sketched his friends. The folds in the fabric, the hands, the expression of the eyes, everything had to reflect reality. At this time, he sketched both Sarah Bernhardt and the playwright Sardou, little knowing how important a role they would have in his future.

Mucha's next important venture was an invitation to produce a calendar for the publishers Lorrilleux. He was to be paid a substantial sum of money: 2500 francs. Lorrilleux was a well-known paint manu-facturer and the commission brought yet another welcome wave of publicity. The calendar was published in 1892 and distributed to art schools, theatres and individual painters. The twelve drawings depicted children, enclosed within a circular framework, each playing with the signs of the zodiac. Mucha employed traditional Renaissance motifs in the style of Makart, but again, the work was predictable in both style and quality.

His successes brought numerous visitors to his room in rue de Chaumière. It was here that he met Gauguin and later, Strindberg.

Moet & Chandon Champagne White Star, 1899 (Private collection). Mucha's track record as a gifted illustrator was now well established. He drew advertisements for many high-profile clients. This particular poster is one of two very beautiful designs for the most famous French manufacturers of champagne.

Moet & Chandon Champagne Dry Imperial, *c.* **1899** (Private collection). The second of Mucha's famous designs for Moet & Chandon.

Mucha was a popular figure in the neighbourhood. Many of the pupils he had studied with at the Académie Julian and at the Académie Colarossi regularly called on him to ask his advice. He was a warm, sympathetic, prepossessing, handsome young man, who found it hard to refuse any request. He would correct the work of his visitors, recommend improvements, give them homework and encourage people to call in at their leisure. Sharing his knowledge with others was an important ingredient of his day-to-day routine and it eventually became a crucial part of his life. It was not long, however, before he found himself running dangerously short of time and he struggled to honour his own work commitments. His inability to restrict the number of callers meant that he was forced to work long into the night. He would take on board far too many commissions, always under-estimating the length of time involved to complete them.

His proudest accomplishment of this period was his contribution to Charles Seignobos' *Scènes et episodes de l'histoire d'Allemagne.* Mucha had always been attracted to the idea of historical painting. Seignobos' history of Germany, although it did not explore the history of his own homeland, was an irresistible commission involving extensive historical research and an individual artistic interpretation of that history. Mucha energetically plunged himself into this work, which was to occupy him until 1898. While completing the project, he became dangerously ill. His memoirs do not indicate the cause of the illness, but it may well have been typhoid. He was forced to travel to Hustopece to recuperate. His drawings for Seignobos were postponed and could not be finished before the stated deadline. He was unable to draw or paint and he was desperately short of money. Eventually he returned to Paris and wrote pleading notes to Henri Bourrelier, begging for help and explaining his problems. It was now December 1894, and he had no way of affording the trip back to Moravia for Christmas. He was obliged to remain in Paris and watch many of his friends journey abroad to the comforts of home life with their families.

Fate intervened once again to rescue Mucha from his despair. One afternoon, shortly before Christmas, a friend came to lunch at Madame Charlotte's. Kadar wanted to go back home for the festive season, but he had some unfinished work to attend to at the Lemercier printing house. Knowing that Mucha could certainly do with the extra income, Kadar asked his friend whether or not he would consider covering for him while he was away. With no particular place to go to, and now urgently in need of extra money, Mucha agreed to complete the work which Kadar could not finish. The Lemercier printing house was situated in the rue de Seine, very close to where Mucha was living. The firm had earned its name printing calendars, decorative menus, leaflets and some posters, designed by quite famous artists, including Puvis de Chavannes and de Feure. Mucha was not unknown to the proprietors of this firm. He had already undertaken several very small lithographic jobs for them and had established himself as a dependable and speedy draughtsman. He felt quite comfortable with the idea of checking proofs for his friend.

On the afternoon of St Stephen's Day 1894, Mucha was busy correcting proofs when the telephone rang. The manager of the Théâtre de Renaissance was on the end of the line. He wanted to know if anyone was available to design a poster as quickly as possible. Sarah Bernhardt, their leading actress and a household theatrical name in Paris, had expressed her unhappiness with a poster which had been produced for her forthcoming play *Gismonda*. She was demanding a replacement poster and stipulated that it should be ready for display by New Year's Day. Monsieur de Brunoff, who managed the Lemercier printing works and valued the custom of this great actress, was thrown into panic. Most of his skilled draughtsmen were away for the entire holiday. As a last resort, Brunoff turned to Mucha and asked him whether he might consider trying his hand at designing a poster. It was a considerable risk for the firm. Mucha had never done such work before, he had no experience in the field of poster design, but he rose enthusiastically to the challenge. He had very little to lose in terms of artistic reputation, and, besides, he had a lot of time on his hands which he earnestly wished to put to good use.

CHAPTER 2

Parisian Fame

The theatre played an immensely important part in European society towards the close of the last century. As there were no cinemas or television screens, it was an invaluable source of entertainment and one of its most powerful exponents was actress Sarah Bernhardt.

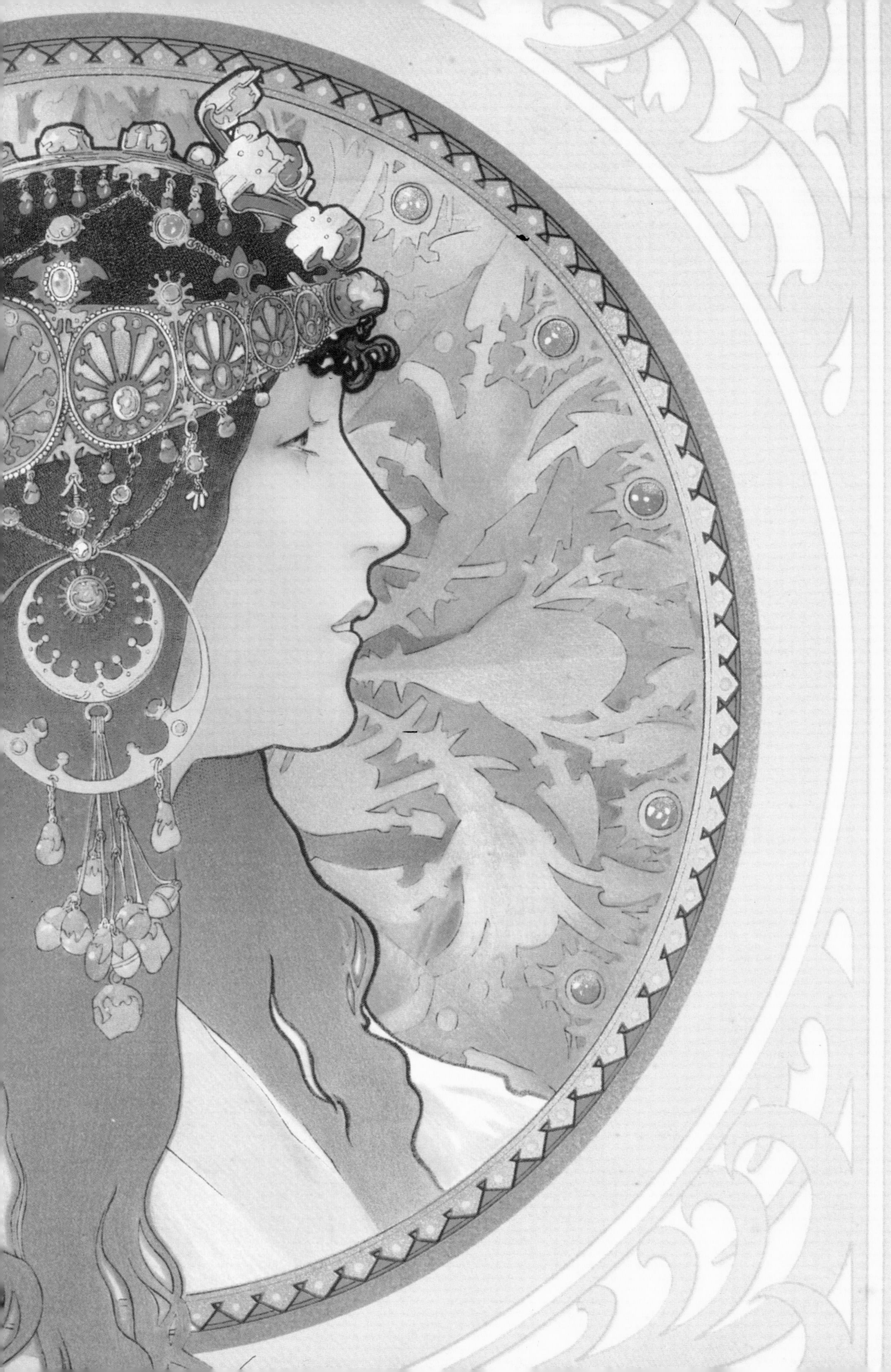

For those who were fortunate enough to see her theatrical performances, Sarah Bernhardt was considered to be much more than an actress. She was a living legend, a woman who possessed an hypnotic power over her audience – charming, beautiful, triumphant, inexhaustible, versatile, dedicated – she personified a new strain of femininity, she represented an enviable female figure. Mucha's overnight rise to fame was the direct result of his association with Bernhardt and she became the genuine inspiration for his original style. The poster Mucha designed for Bernhardt's leading role in Sardou's play, *Gismonda*, was the first of many he painted for her and it heralded a long, satisfying relationship which was to span many successfully creative years.

Having decided to attempt to satisfy the demands of the Théâtre de Renaissance at such short notice, Mucha and his employer Brunoff made their way to meet with Sarah Bernhardt. Mucha was uncomfortable to find himself among so many famous, well-dressed people, but he soon settled down to sketching scenes from the play, from which he intended to select his poster design. It was a help to him that he could sympathize with the content of Sardou's play. He felt at ease with the Byzantine setting of the drama; it exuded a familiar atmosphere, reminding him of his childhood in Moravia. Various artists had drawn posters for Sarah before now, including Eugene Grasset. The publicity value of an association with Sarah was undeniably great, but this did not seem to concern Mucha. He had always been modest and utterly lacking in conceit. He simply got on with the task before him. 'I sketched her dress, the golden flowers in her hair, the wide sleeves, and a palm leaf in her hand,' he noted later.

Mucha concentrated on the Byzantine richness of his surroundings, on Sarah's beautiful embroidered garment and on the glorious sovereignty of her female form. He agreed with the theatre manager to produce quickly a full-sized drawing of Sarah for his approval. He drew the upper part straight on to one lithographic stone and while this was being printed, he drew the lower part on another stone. It was a very rushed job, the lower stone was taken away before Mucha had a chance to finish the detail of the design, so that the poster appears slightly imbalanced. By 30 December, the work had been completed and hung up to dry. Brunoff was extremely nervous of the result, which was so radically different from anything previously presented to the theatre by the Lemercier firm. He was most reluctant to show the poster to Bernhardt, but had no other option. Sarah, however, was absolutely thrilled with what she saw. She ordered the posters to be printed and distributed. They were seen by the public on the first day of January 1895 and caused quite a sensation.

Before Mucha appeared on the artistic scene, posters had largely been painted in the old style, using naturalistic detail and allegorical

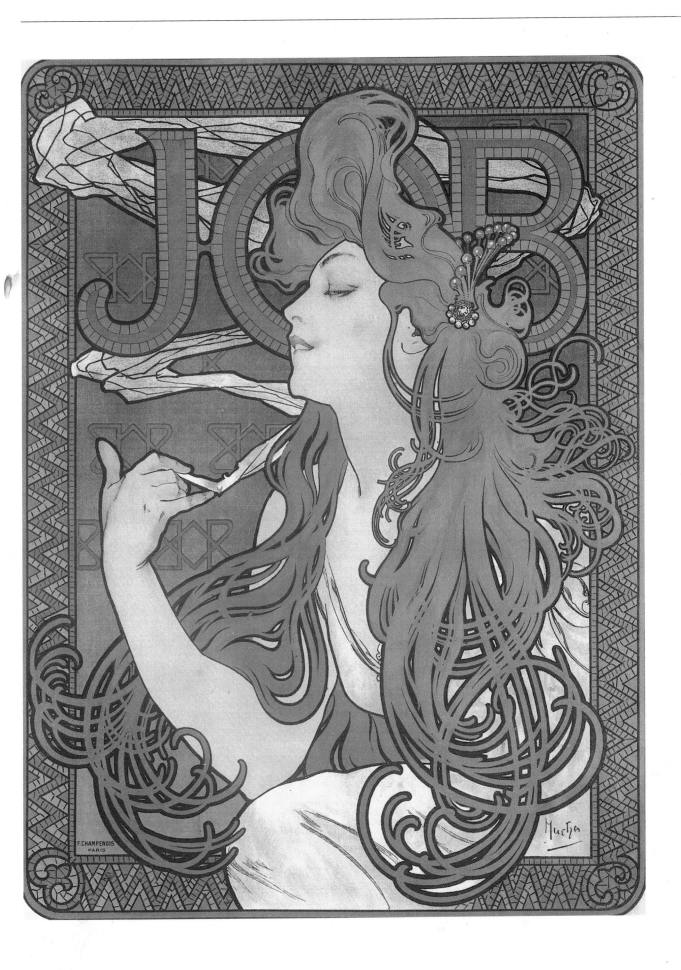

The **Job** poster Mucha produced in 1898 favours a more russet colour scheme and has a distinctly oriental flavour. Again, the hair is an immediately striking feature, cascading in circular swoops of the pencil from the head right down to the model's delicate, bare feet (Private collection).

IMP. F. CHAMPENOIS. 66.Boulᵗ Sᵗ MICHEL. PARIS

figures. As early as 1866, Chéret had introduced his own peculiar brand of poster art to the French public, attempting to redress the distinct lack of imagination of previous models. Chéret was extremely successful and might certainly be held accountable for the decisive revolution which occurred in advertising. His work was so striking that advertisement pillars, for the first time, grabbed the attention of passers-by. Unlike Mucha however, Chéret used fiery colours, especially an abundance of red, and preferred naturalistic figures in his work.

Grasset was another artist who produced posters. His *Joan of Arc* has often been compared with Mucha's *Gismonda*. Some accused Mucha of imitating Grasset's art, especially his floral designs, rich decoration and stained-glass window effect. Mucha had a great respect for Grasset, but there was nothing new about Grasset's art. Mucha did not seek to reproduce his style, rather to develop it further, adding his own inspiration and introducing the originality Grasset lacked. He managed to do this very successfully, bringing about a remarkable fusion of his own ideals and a proficiency of technique inherited from his predecessors. Jiri Mucha, Mucha's son, often watched his father at work. His biography, *Alphonse Maria Mucha*, is an invaluable guide to the methods of the artist:

He would begin by breaking up the area with the principal design. Then he would immediately fill the vacant areas with more lines, at first only with a few so as not to upset the balance, then more and more, developing them simultaneously until the whole became a harmonious pattern of curves and arabesques. He never had a pre-conceived plan and never concentrated on a single area of the picture. His hand moved firmly over the paper, every new line leading to others out of a simple sense of balance.

Gismonda is arguably the most impressive poster Mucha ever produced. The two separately lithographed images were joined together to form a life-size poster, seven feet high. Mucha had no experience of designing such a large-scale work and it is astounding that he managed it with such skill and dexterity. The sketches Mucha made at the theatre deviate only slightly from the end result, but there is one striking difference. He decided to remove any traces of red colouring from his poster. The subtle, muted, melting tones which allow for the enhancement of his highly refined draughtsmanship signalled a completely new departure for this genre. Wherever luminous colours were used, they took up only a tiny amount of space. Mucha's great gift was his remarkable feel for colour, his ability to employ subtle mixtures of violet, gold, green and shades of brown, in order to produce the most harmonious effect possible.

Jerome Doucet, in the *Revue Illustrée*, was among several critics who wrote enthusiastically about Mucha's first great public work:

This poster, this white window, this mosaic on the wall, is a creation of the first order which has well deserved its triumph ... It seemed ... when Chéret was covering our walls with posters, each more beautiful than the last, that nobody would be able to exhibit along-side him in the Salon de la Rue. We feared ... that our houses would be plunged into mourning, because neither Grasset's diplomas, nor the rare decorations of Toulouse-Lautrec, could have filled the void left by Chéret. But now – behold – another artist has come along, worthy to take his place and win the approval of the hurrying, choosy Parisians. Mucha has triumphed where success seemed impossible. It is the triumph of silk, gold and precious stones, it is the wealth thrown open-handed on the dubious whiteness of our city's walls.

The poster *Gismonda*, like the many which followed, is an exquisite celebration of feminine beauty. It has a distinctive, entirely novel, elongated shape which Mucha used again and again while working with Sarah Bernhardt. The actress is portrayed in profile, standing dreamily in a beautiful, ornate costume, painted in shades of turquoise and gold. She holds a palm leaf in her hand and, behind her, in the upper portion of the poster, her name is inscribed within the arc of a typanum. Circular features occur repeatedly in Mucha's work. His predilection for Baroque curves and undulating lines is obvious in most of his art. Curves and swirls are used by him in the decorative transformation of hair, for example. Critics often used the description 'macaroni hair' to describe the Medusa-like tendrils of hair frequently depicted in his art. In this poster, Sarah's hair is dressed with flowers; she is a natural, flowing form, yet 'transformed' in the spirit of *art nouveau*. The upper background is decorated in a style reminiscent of a Byzantine mosaic, filled in with tiny square tiles of stone or glass producing a *tesserae* effect. Mucha's female form demands to be worshipped, which is precisely the effect Sarah Bernhardt desired to achieve.

Gismonda won the admiration of most Parisian spectators. In the eyes of the Paris public, Mucha had succeeded in popularizing a new fledgling art form which, until now, had been tentatively christened *art nouveau*. After the appearance of Mucha's poster, *art nouveau* was often referred to as *Le Style Mucha*, but Mucha refused to wear this label, insisting that he painted only what he personally believed in. *Art nouveau* was a movement which nominally arrived with the exhibition at Bing's *Maison de l'Art Nouveau* in 1895. Mucha was immediately associated with the movement, and it's certainly true that he displayed some of its characteristics: he favoured sensuous subject matter, usually female, and fluid forms; he painted in rich arabesques and milky, subdued tones; he used classical models, and refused to honour naturalistic portraits. This was typical of the *art nouveau* school, whose adherents believed that truth to nature could also be expressed in the correctness of the artistic structure created.

Monaco · Monte-Carlo was the most glamorous holiday poster ever produced in France advertising railway tickets to Monte Carlo. The poster is brimming with circular motifs, from aureoles to crescent shapes. It is one of the few posters where Mucha uses red tones, but he does so sparingly and skilfully with great dramatic effect (Private collection).

MONACO · MONTE-CARLO

Mucha transformed his females into glorious figures. He insisted, however, that his subject matter and sensitivity to colour were derived from nature; decorative bands and floral motifs were borrowed from folk embroidery. He believed there was nothing so repugnant as painting in the style of a fashionable school. A spiritual message, inherent in the picture, was the only possible justification of art. The artist existed, above all, to spread light. Mucha never spoke about *art nouveau* and regularly used the phrase: 'I did it in my own way.' His son Jiri records, however, how difficult it was for Mucha to divorce himself from the whole *art nouveau* movement: 'It was a paradox characteristic of my father's life that again and again that aspect of his art which was most conditioned by fashion brought him most fame ... for him his work was simply art, and his personal gift to draw and paint.'

After the first collaboration with Sarah Bernhardt, there followed a six-year contract with her until she departed for America in 1901. The contract Sarah drew up with Mucha was not limited to the production of posters. He agreed to design sets, to advise on costumes, to create new jewellery and to generally assist, when required, in the production and direction of her plays. Sarah Bernhardt was an incredibly shrewd businesswoman and she had every reason to be pleased with her new protégé. In 1896, she had already fought and won a court case with Lemercier over the *Gismonda* poster. She very quickly realized that *Gismonda* was fast becoming a collector's item and had ordered and paid for 4000 copies of the poster in advance, at less than a franc each. When Lemercier failed to deliver the final 550 posters, she sued the company, refusing to accept a cash hand-out in lieu of the posters. The court case proved a major catastrophe for Lemercier, the firm lost all future orders from the actress. Bernhardt rapidly transferred her affairs to the publisher Champenois.

Mucha signed a new contract, which effectively made him the exclusive property of his new agent. Under Champenois, he was quickly made to revise his understanding of the word commercialism.

Other projects with Sarah quickly followed *Gismonda*. The evolution of Mucha's style into something quite unique owed a considerable amount to Sarah Bernhardt's sheer magnetism and physical attraction. Bernhardt's next play, *La Princesse Lointaine,* was written by Edmond Rostand. There was simply no time to create a poster for this production, so Mucha designed instead a spectacular programme based on drawings of the sets at rehearsal. The crown of lilies adorning Sarah's head became an emblem of *art nouveau*. As a result of the play's tremendous popularity, Mucha received an offer from the publisher Piazza to illustrate a work similar to Rostand's play, to be entitled *Ilsée*. Champenois was also making demands on his time. He commissioned Mucha to design a series of *panneaux* for commercial sale to the public. The *panneaux* were decorative panels, produced in a narrow, elongated

Paul Verola's **Rama**, a drama in verse, was published in 1898 by the Bibliothèque Artistique et Litteraire. Mucha designed five full-colour illustrations for the book (Private collection).

There are fewer signs of purely decorative elements in *Rama* compared to *Ilsée*. Mucha concentrated instead on conveying the emotions of the protagonists (Private collection).

format, rather like the posters, but without any text. Jiri has again recorded the technique Mucha used for these *panneaux*:

> *My father first drew the designs in coloured pencil, pastel, or occasionally watercolour. Several variants exist of many of the designs, since in his thoroughness he continued experimenting*

until he was entirely satisfied. Then he drew the panel full size on tracing paper and transferred the drawing from this on to the stone. The press produced several monochrome proofs, and not until then did he start using colour. He did this in order to avoid having to draw everything again from the beginning whenever some colour variation displeased him. The final colour original was thus a tinted monochrome print. After this stage came the colour proofs, the corrections and the printing on silk. This system of tracing drawings was used by Mucha again later, in the painting of large format pictures.

Some of the *panneaux* were printed on silk or satin cloth, others on superior quality paper. Mucha's first *panneaux* were a representation of the four seasons of the year. They were a huge commercial success and many re-prints were demanded. The quality of the *panneaux* varied dramatically as a result. Mucha did not always have the time to supervise the print-runs and some of the *panneaux* were not correctly reproduced. On a number of occasions the clarity of line and colour was compromised, but this did not at all affect Champenois' profit of purse. The publisher had promised Mucha a regular annual salary, a promise he duly honoured, but he was offering Mucha a form of slavery at the same time. Mucha's workload was overwhelming; he was swamped by a flood of commissions. He had not yet finished his illustrations for Seignobos' *Scenes et episodes de l'histoire d'Allemagne* and had already promised to work on a similar history of Spain. He was due to deliver more posters and *panneaux* to Champenois, including the poster *Salon des Cent*. He was still completing the drawings for *Ilsée* and, in the midst of all his work commitments, he was forced to transport all his belongings to a much larger studio.

Mucha moved to the rue Val-de-Grâce in the summer of 1896. He decorated his new home in a style of Byzantine extravagance. The walls were draped with red brocade, furniture was of a strange, oriental design, there were Persian rugs on the floor and numerous vases of flowers casually placed around the rooms. Incense sticks burned fragrantly beneath a carving of the Virgin Mary. Paul Redonnel, writer for *La Plume*, presented a good contemporary description of Mucha's studio in his *avant-garde* magazine:

It makes the impression of a secular chapel ... screens placed here and there that could well be confessionals; and then there's incense burning all the time. It's more like the chapel of an Oriental monk than a studio.

Mucha immediately began preparing for the new season of the Théâtre de la Renaissance. Sarah returned from America and opened the season on 30 September with *La Dame aux Camelias*. Mucha designed the poster for this play, a work which resembled an intricate water-colour rather than an advertisement, with its rich decorative contrasts in the scattering of silver stars on the violet twilight sky behind the figure of the lady with the camellias. The poster displays an astoundingly sensitive balance of colour and form. Mucha followed this with another poster for *Lorenzaccio*.

From 1896 to 1902, although he felt he was being unmercifully exploited by Champenois, he still managed to produce many of his best works and his impact on the world of art and fashion was strongest during these years. Paris had embraced *art nouveau* with a vibrant passion. Fashion mimicked the ideals of the movement. Ladies' gowns flowed in sumptuous folds, the natural curves of the female form were no longer subject to the corset. Paris had taught Mucha sophistication, polish and realism of technique. He painted a poster for *Les Amants* in March 1896, which was uncharacteristically horizontal in composition, showing groups of figures, rather than a single, central subject. The best of Mucha's *panneaux* were all conceived in rue Val-de-Grâce, including the *Four Jewels, Four Stars, Four Arts* and *Four Times of Day*. Champenois had discovered a new way of exploiting Mucha's talent, by either printing everything Mucha produced in a reduced size, or selling the rights to do this to the highest bidder. The *panneaux decoratifs* were reproduced time and time again as posters, calendars and even postcards. Mucha also completed advertisements for the champagne firm Ruinart, and for Moet & Chandon's *Dry Imperial* champagne. He produced the famous travel poster *Monaco·Monte-Carlo* in 1897 and made drawings advertising toothpaste, cigarette-papers and Nestlé's baby food. He painted the superb *Job* posters in 1896 and 1898.

Apart from lithographic works, Mucha also produced some very fine book illustrations during this time. He finally completed Robert De Fler's *Ilsée, Princesse de Tripoli*, in 1897. This work displays an astonishing decorative talent on virtually every page, in spite of the fact that the arrival of De Fler's manuscript left Mucha with only three months in which to complete 134 coloured lithographs. He also illustrated Paul Verola's *Rama* in 1898 and Anatole France's *Clio*, published in 1900. *Le Pater* which he felt was superior to *Ilsée*, was commissioned by Piazza and consisted of a book of commentaries and pictorial interpretations of the Lord's Prayer. It was eventually published in 1899.

He devoted any spare time he possibly could to teaching. In 1897, he formed a teaching partnership with the American artist Whistler, and taught at the local Académie Carmen. Whistler, although a puritan in many ways, was the first of his artistic friends to articulate openly what were also Mucha's inherent fears, that he was not following the

Clio, **1900**. This was published by Claman Levy in a limited edition of 150 copies and became a collector's item almost immediately. It is an excellent example of Mucha's talent for book illustration, a side of his work which he thoroughly enjoyed, yet one which is often overlooked (Private collection).

true path of an artist. Whistler criticized the etherealized women Mucha painted in his work, informing him that they could not possibly represent the proper subject of art. He advised Mucha to turn to the streets for inspiration, to real people and real experiences. Fame however, was not ready to release him just yet.

Mucha's studio in rue Val-de-Grâce rapidly became one of the most fashionable haunts in Paris. He socialized here with all sorts of people, including scientists, mystics and especially other artists. Yet, for all his love of Paris society, he remained strangely inaccessible to women. Rumours circulated that he was having an affair with Sarah, but those who knew him well laughed at the suggestion. Mucha had far too much respect for Sarah to contemplate such a thing. Although he was born into the Catholic religion and remained a Catholic all his life, Mucha was attracted to the occult and to esoteric philosophies in general. Through a contact, Albert de Rochas, he met with the astronomer Flammarion in the late 1890s and their friendship lasted a great many years. Flammarion would hold séances in Mucha's studio, which had been converted into a form of psychic laboratory, and de Rochas would write about them in the journal *La Nature*. During the séances, Mucha made contact with the spirit world and especially his dead relatives, asking their advice on which direction he should take in his art. He was often seen transcribing their words to him in a number of different languages.

Mucha's day would begin at nine in the morning and end well after midnight. His memoirs communicate an accurate picture of the scene that greeted an artist of his popularity as soon as he awoke:

> *Sometimes there was quite a crowd, sometimes a smaller gathering, but never fewer than ten people trying to sell me books or costumes, publishers offering me work or bringing proofs for correction ... in spite of the notice I had put up, that I received only between five and seven in the evening. But foreigners always had the excuse that they were just leaving Paris, they would not keep me long, all they wanted was a signed photograph or something similar.*

At this time, he was also involved with a number of artists connected with the *La Plume* magazine, edited by Leon Deschamps – a publication strictly within the spirit of *art nouveau*. The group of artists included, amongst others, Grasset, Bonnard, de Feure and Toulouse-Lautrec. Mucha's reputation had grown enormously and it may well have been this very group that persuaded him it was high time he introduced his work to the public. In early 1897, Mucha's artistic achievements were put on show in the first of two exhibitions that year. The exhibition which opened on 15 February was organized by the *Journal des Artistes* at 18 rue Saint-Lazare, *à la Bodinière*, where

Opposite:
Mucha's famous pale colouring dominates his illustrations for *Clio*. He uses shades of turquoise, green and creamy yellow to achieve a sobering effect (Private collection).

Mucha's admiration for Anatole France whom he considered a logical and clear-thinking philosopher is reflected in the illustrations for *Clio*. He produced fourteen drawings in total for the work (Private collection).

Steinlen and other leading poster designers had already successfully exhibited their work. Mucha's best posters and *panneaux*, including the *Four Seasons*, were put on display to the public. Twenty-seven of the illustrations for *Episodes de l'Histoire de l'Allemagne* were shown, together with various drawings for calendars, menus, and a single oil painting. The gallery owners were very keen to exploit Mucha's association with Sarah Bernhardt and he was asked to encourage her to write a piece which might introduce the exhibition catalogue. Sarah's letter to her young artist friend was reproduced in the opening page:

> *Mon bien cher Mucha,*
> *You ask me to present you to the Parisian public. Well, my dear friend, follow my advice: exhibit your works, they will speak for you, I know my dear Parisian public. The delicacy of your drawing, the originality of your composition, the lovely colours of your posters and pictures – all this will charm them, and after your exhibition I predict fame for you.*
> *My two hands in yours, my dear Mucha, SB.*

The second, much more prestigious exhibition, ran from May to July 1897, at the Salon des Cent, 31 rue Bonaparte, the gallery of the journal *La Plume*. Over four hundred items were put on display, two-thirds of which were completed by the artist within the previous two years. As the reviews revealed, Mucha had won the hearts of the Paris public; he had convinced the gallery visitors beyond all doubt that he was an exceptional draughtsman, a master of the *art nouveau* style. A few prominent critics even put forward the suggestion that he should be nominated to design the automobile. Mucha expressed

Clio was a masterpiece and perfectly in keeping with the fashion of the times. Each illustration was surrounded by a wide margin, as if the intention were to frame a very rare painting (Private collection).

two disappointments with these exhibitions. The first regret was that few of the critics had paid any attention to his 'serious' work. Their concentration was focused on his decorative work, which he was beginning to despise, yet for which, ironically, he is best remembered. The second disappointment arose from the fact that these same critics persisted in describing him as Hungarian. The deliberate oversight prompted the publication of a letter in the newspaper *La Francel*. It was signed SB, and reiterated for the French public, in no uncertain terms, that Mucha was a Czech citizen, an artist whose roots filled him with pride.

He was slowly becoming impatient with all of his work of the *art nouveau* period. Subconsciously, he had already begun to divorce himself from the movement. By the time he had painted *La Plume* and *Primavère* in 1899, the spontaneity and vulnerability of his earlier compositions was replaced by a tougher attitude. In these later works, his style is slightly more clinical and more dependent on the repetition of standard motifs. Only a few of his later posters, for example, *Princess Hyacinth*, printed in 1911, move towards recapturing the charming, innocent sexuality of his earlier work in Paris. By now, he was inundated with requests to design all sorts of objects, from jewellery, to furniture, from fabric patterns to ceramics. He was increasingly unhappy with his inability to pursue a grander art. He expressed his frustration in his journal:

> I saw my work adorning the salons of the highest society or flattering people of the great world with smiling and ennobled portraits. I saw the books full of legendary scenes, floral garlands and drawings glorifying the beauty and tenderness of women. This was what my time, my precious time, was being spent on, when my nation was left to quench its thirst on ditch water.

There is little of the symbolic ornamentation in these drawings, so apparent in the illustrations for **Ilsée**. Much of the background remains bare, an exercise in restraint for Mucha which produces a style of art complementary to the clear, often despondent prose of Anatole France (Private collection).

CHAPTER 3

Realities and Desires

The nineteenth century was rapidly drawing to a close. The industrialization of the Western world was firmly under way. Many changes were taking place at an alarming rate and Paris began to reflect a universal mood of social upheaval.

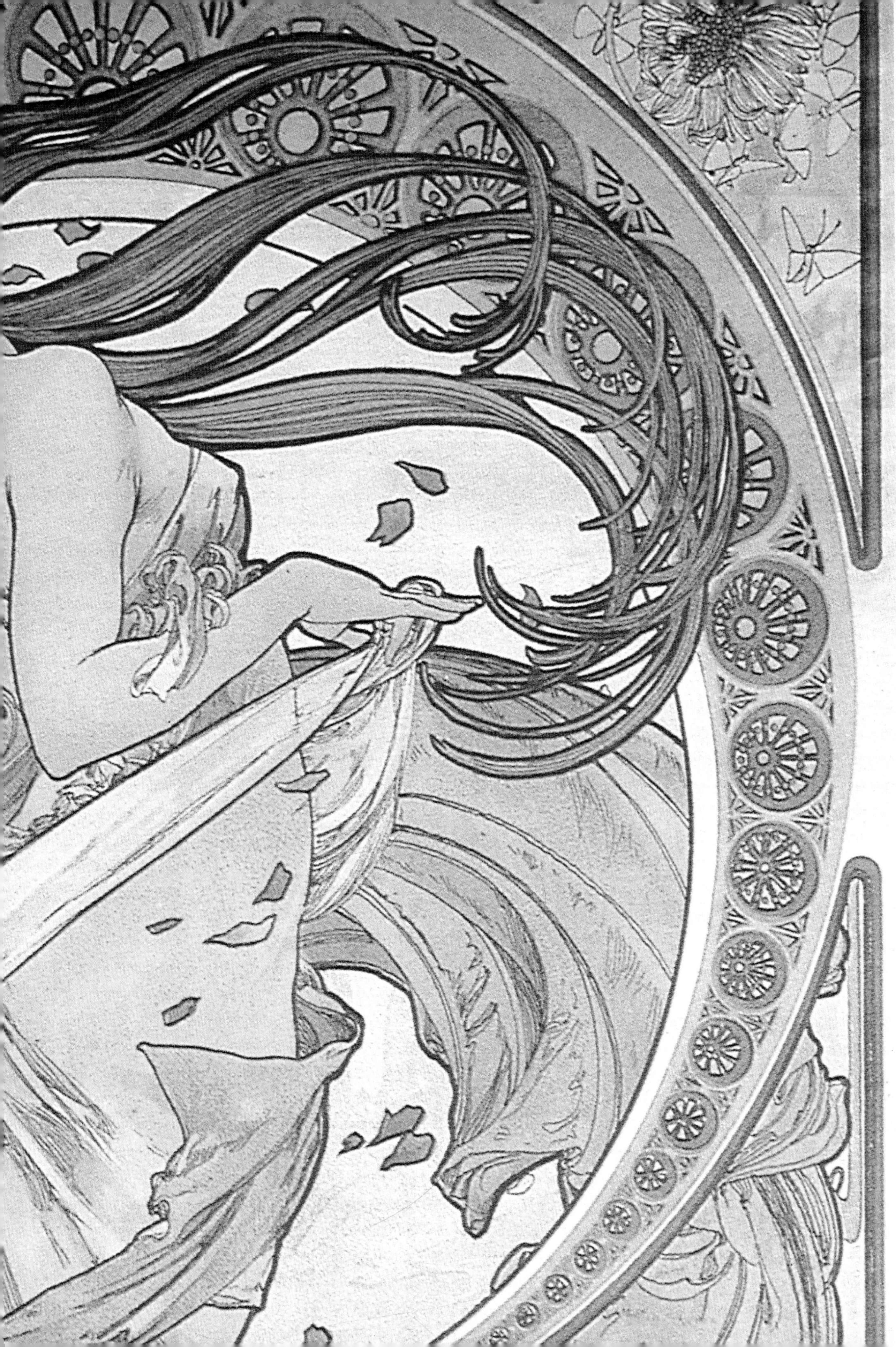

Overleaf:
La Danse belongs to a collection of four exquisite *panneaux* entitled **The Four Arts – Dance, Poetry, Painting and Music**. These were drawn in 1898 while Mucha was living at rue Val-de-Grâce (Private collection).

It was a time of memorable scientific progress. Mucha was passionately interested in science and he paid serious attention to the discoveries of modern scientists. In 1900, the first Metro station opened in Paris, cinematography was undergoing its first public trials, Santos-Dumont's airships hovered in the Parisian sky, and Marconi was waiting to transmit his first wireless signal. Meanwhile, the halls for the great Paris Exhibition, which would attract hundreds of thousands of visitors from every conceivable corner of the earth, were being erected on the banks of the river Seine. The great Paris Exhibition of 1900 was intended to signify a gateway to the future.

Mucha became involved in the planning of the Exhibition from its earliest stages, although quite how he managed this remains somewhat of a mystery. He was forty years old, people around him were changing, an entire era was about to fade away. He treated his involvement as part of his search for a way forward, yet he was engaged in a whole range of other projects while the Exhibition was taking shape. He still worked at the Théâtre de la Renaissance and was in the process of drawing the poster for Sarah's new Rostand play, *L'Aiglon*. The pressures of too many work commitments undoubtedly contributed to the uncharacteristically inferior quality of this poster. It appears as if Mucha's unfinished sketch, hastily coloured, was enlarged and sent to print without final approval. In the rush up to the Exhibition, he probably did not have the time to supervise the project satisfactorily. He had begun his painting *Quo Vadis* at this time also, which was to occupy him, with many interruptions, for the next ten years. He had only just completed *The Lord's Prayer*, and he was still producing commercial art for Champenois, from *panneaux* to posters, to magazine covers.

He had begun to sculpt at this time. The sculptor Seysses lived on the ground floor beneath Mucha's studio in rue Val-de-Grâce and the two men became acquainted. Mucha collaborated with Seysses on some of his sculptures and quickly developed his own talent. He became a close friend of Rodin, who encouraged him to abandon his commercial obligations to Champenois and to move on to a different, more rewarding medium. The best known of Mucha's sculptures is the bronze bust *La Nature*. It was conceived in the *art nouveau* style. The hair of the female figure meanders in serpentine coils, spiralling over naked breasts to the waistline. The face has an ethereal beauty and is languidly peaceful. Many consider the bust to be a portrait of Sarah Bernhardt, but it may equally be the face of any number of Mucha's female models, resembling, in particular, the head of one of the young girls in the *Zodiac* calendar. The bust was exhibited at the Paris Exhibition as part of the Austrian collection of art.

By 1900, Mucha had almost had his fill of *art nouveau*, but the Exhibition was to be its most triumphant pageant ever. It impressed

itself deeply on the imagination of all who visited and the event was elevated to legendary status. Each country, each race, exhibited of its own free will in a gigantic, magnificent venue, ablaze with thousands of electric lightbulbs. Bands continued to play while the night sky erupted with spectacular fireworks. Each nation competed for the spectator's attention. The visitor might decide to visit an Eastern temple, or admire the beauty of Chinese lanterns and silk dolls; he could delight in the lavishly decorated pavilions, sit through a talking film, or even attempt to transmit with wireless signals.

The Four Flowers *panneaux* painted in
1897 beautifully represents the **Iris,
Carnation, Lily** and **Rose**.
(Private collection).

Mucha decorated the *Bosnian Pavilion* for the Paris Exhibition. Nothing, unfortunately, remains of the pavilion today; it was dismantled after the Exhibition and the drawings were lost. Mucha also undertook to design some of the amazing tapestries adorning the monumental gates leading to the Austrian exhibition, for which he won a gold medal. He decorated the presentation chamber for the perfume firm Houbigant. Jean de la Tour wrote a description of this chamber in *Le Figaro* magazine:

> *The display room of the Houbigant company was decorated by Maestro Mucha who created a flowery apotheosis of a perfumery: frames over which climb cobaea, wisteria and mimosa. There are four panels symbolizing the most important plants of the perfume industry: the rose, the violet, orange blossom and the yellow buttercup ... Four small display cases, also designed by Mucha, contain bottles of Houbigant perfumes, and in the middle of the room there is a statue of a young girl rising from a wreath of irises, violets and roses.*

One of his most ambitious projects for the Exhibition never came to fruition. It was Mucha's intention, one he shared with many other architects, to build a permanent pavilion known as *The Pavilion of Man*. The plan was to dismantle the Eiffel Tower, down to the first platform, and then re-build it in an entirely different way. The new pavilion was to remain a permanent structure and the project would be a vast undertaking. Mucha's first design consisted of a building adorned with gigantic statues, poised on the bottom part of the Eiffel Tower. A globe was to be positioned at the apex of the building, intended as a mystical monument to Man, beaming wisdom into the whole world. Mucha worked on all the plans, drawings and plaster models, but the project was never realized, probably because of the mammoth cost.

An alternative architectural enterprise presented itself in the wake of this disappointment. The goldsmith Fouquet, an avid admirer of *art nouveau*, was about to open a new shop in Paris' rue Royale, which he wanted decorated in the most modern style possible. Fouquet was a distinguished jeweller in Paris, selling individually modelled pieces of jewellery to a wealthy clientèle. Mucha agreed to design both the interior and the front of the shop. His work for Fouquet formed an important part of his creative life at this time. He was able to employ most of his versatile talents, working with many different materials – wood, glass, fabric, plaster and paint. He designed a wonderful mosaic floor for the interior of the shop, produced beautiful stained-glass *panneaux* and carved elegant furniture in precious wood. In 1920, when Fouquet's shop was closed down, Fouquet's son donated the interior decoration to the Musée Carnavalet in Paris.

Salomé was produced in 1897 for the cover of the revue magazine *L'Estampe Moderne*. Mucha designed the covers of many subsequent issues between May 1897 and April 1899 (Private collection).

Mucha also introduced Fouquet to an original concept of jewellery design, so complex and unusual in shape that many critics were baffled by the artistry. The writer Gustav Kahn described Mucha's influence on the world of jewellery in a 1902 edition of *Art et Décoration*:

> *Mucha brought to jewellery all his awesome gifts of an almost visionary decorator ... He adorned a woman's breast with a necklace combining gems with an ivory miniature that forms the main ingredient of the piece. The pendant, shaped like big golden leaves, is focused around the centrepiece – a girl's head in ivory enhanced by the colour of the cheeks, the lips and the eyes. In his jewellery we again find that sensitive, balanced polychromy, rich in lively colours, that we find in his posters ... each piece is a work of art in miniature, emanating an impression of solidity and strength, just like his stained glass windows and reliefs.*

Most of the jewellery designed by Mucha has disappeared over the years, without trace. A good deal of it was reproduced and copied by other goldsmiths, especially the bracelet in the shape of a snake, studded with diamonds and rubies, that he made for Sarah Bernhardt. It, too, was exhibited at the Paris Exhibition.

Still plagued by endless requests for various designs, Mucha came to the decision to begin work on an encyclopaedia of his artistic achievements. By introducing it as a source of knowledge to artists all over the world, he hoped this reference work might alleviate the pressures of his situation, allowing him to dedicate himself to a much nobler activity which demanded its day.

Documents Décoratifs was issued in 1902 by the Librairie Centrale des Beaux Arts as a volume to instruct students and manufacturers in every branch of decorative and applied art. It included Mucha's commentaries on his *panneaux*, jewellery, stained-glass works, furniture and pottery. There were seventy-two plates, both monochrome and hand-coloured and it became one of the few books on design where even individual plates were considered collector's items. The enterprising publishers distributed it to schools and art academies throughout the world, but still Mucha's situation remained unaltered. If anything, it worsened. He was being pestered for even more advice on style and received even more demands to make or paint items for various people. For Lefèvre-Utilé, he produced the famous poster of Sarah Bernhardt as *La Princesse Lointaine*, as well as a calendar and designs for their biscuits which were either printed directly on to the tins or printed on paper and pasted on. The market was now flooded by mass-produced, inferior replicas of Mucha's work copied on to glass, mosaics and even wallpaper.

Salammbo, 1897 (Private collection) – another of the covers Mucha designed for *L'Estampe Moderne*. This perfectly exemplifies Mucha's early approach, his almost obsessive tendency to decorate every single available space. Note the swirling lines in the background of the drawing clearly in *art nouveau* style.

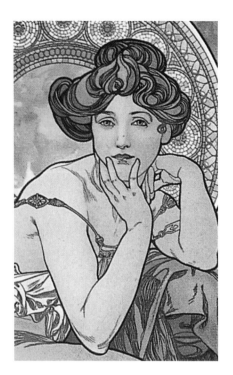

Topaz, from **The Four Jewels**.

Mucha was still frantically searching for the means to spread his light as an artist, still in pursuit of a path leading to something higher. *Art nouveau* was slowly becoming a subject of mockery and Mucha, its main proponent in the eyes of the critics, began to suffer the backlash. *L'Estampe Moderne* was among several journals who began to print disclaiming articles on his artistic worth: 'When one has come to occupy a place and acquire a reputation like Mucha's ... one should neglect the commercial side and aim exclusively to produce art and the truth.'

This was precisely what Mucha had been striving to do all his artistic life. He suffered acutely the injustice of these comments. He had never appreciated the value of money and had never striven to amass great wealth. He was a tortured soul and had been for many years – wrestling against commercialism, making a supreme effort to allocate time to more serious work, desperately longing to make a contribution to his nation.

When Rodin presented him with an invitation to accompany him to the Prague Fine Arts Society Exhibition in 1902, it seemed, at last, that Mucha would have the opportunity to strengthen a neglected relationship with his homeland and discover a way to make amends. He looked forward to meeting fellow Czech artists and to discussing his more serious ambition with them. His popularity as a 'French style' artist of the *art nouveau* school had reached such proportions even abroad, that it was impossible for him to be treated as anything other than that. Mucha had been naïve and idealistic. He had entirely misjudged the response he would receive in his native land. Huge crowds awaited his arrival in Prague and in every single town he visited with Rodin on the trip. Both men were treated as Parisian celebrities. His fellow countrymen were in no way prepared to offer him the chance of a new beginning.

His claim that he was a Czech artist was rejected almost everywhere. He was accepted as a Czech citizen, his nation was proud that he repeatedly emphasized his nationality to his admirers, but he meant nothing whatsoever to Czech art. Czechoslovakian artists stood firm in their opinion that he was a Frenchman who could have nothing of value to say to them on their subject. It did not help to smooth relations when Mucha unleashed a campaign of criticism against his countrymen's art. In France, he had been invited by the Mayor of Paris to deliver his expert opinion on the state of the nation's artistic achievements, with the result that he now felt qualified to do the same in Czechoslovakia. His words met with bitter anger and resentment. Mucha stubbornly pronounced that Czech art had fallen victim to foreign German influence. He was shocked and disappointed by what he saw around him. He accused the Austrian government of enforcing a programme of denationalization of the country's art:

Whenever Austria exhibited at international exhibitions in Vienna ... it usually happened that the works of the Poles, Czechs or Hungarians attracted more interest than those of the German artists, and it was the Slavs who gained most of the medals and awards ... Of course, such a situation seemed unacceptable and humiliating to Austria. The matter was taken in hand by a leading official in the Ministry of Education who wasted no time in arriving at a solution. Realizing that decentralization was harmful to Vienna, he simply centralized it and established a uniform Austrian art.

In Mucha's opinion, art based on old national traditions had all but disappeared. Czechoslovakian art institutions had been poisoned, they had become anchorless, fumbling in all directions, clutching at anything which could be borrowed from neighbouring countries. He was passionate and enraged: 'When in fifty years a historian comes to write the history of art, he will dryly observe that since 1900 the Czech nation has had no art of its own.'

The breach which developed between Mucha and his artistic peers in Czechoslovakia never managed to heal itself, in spite of the great efforts he made in later years to win the approval and recognition of these men. The trip was highly productive in one respect, however. Mucha's soul-searching had finally ceased. He was now resolved to devote himself to a great work for the Slav people. The image was quite clear in his mind. The project would be entitled *The Slav Epic*, a work illustrating the troubled history of the Slavic race, to be painted on monumental canvases and dedicated to his homeland.

Life could never be that simple. He had not stopped to consider how he would possibly gather together the funds to complete such a venture. Now that he was back in Paris, harsh realities refused to be ignored. He was hugely successful and had earned vast amounts of money over the years. He found himself, nonetheless, in dire straits financially. He could have saved quite large amounts during his days of Parisian fame, but he had never managed to do this. He was useless at keeping accounts and his proper judgement of people was marred by his excessive spirit of generosity. People exploited him in order to make their way in society. So-called friends treated him as a cash flow facility. He often paid their bills and allowed them to help themselves to large amounts of his money which he kept in a drawer by his drawing-board.

He was forced to carry on with much the same work as before, all the time rebelling against the routine which he followed for profit. His mood of despair began to creep into his painting. By 1903, his graphic output had diminished considerably and he began to move away from decorative art. He had grown tired of painting florid women in romantic

Emerald, from **The Four Jewels**.

overleaf:
The Four Jewels – Topaz, Emerald, Amethyst and Ruby are a later collection of *panneaux*, painted in 1900. They reveal the level of sophistication Mucha had reached in his art. The clarity of his drawing had reached a peak of excellence, the use of more vibrant colour producing the splendid harmonious effect for which he had become famous (Private collection).

LA TOPAZE

L'ÉMERAUDE

L'AMÉTHYSTE

LE RUBIS

Amethyst, from **The Four Jewels**.

settings, he could no longer express the inner equilibrium of his earlier paintings. In private, he painted obese, drunken whores instead of beautiful women. A poster he designed for Sarah Bernhardt at this time for her play *La Sorcière* was never used. He suffered a terrible setback when an order for the Jerusalem panels was cancelled. This series of murals, commissioned by the Prior of Jerusalem, was intended to adorn the walls of the Chapel of the Virgin Mary. Mucha was to paint the compositions on location, based on the liturgy of the Old and New Testaments. He had made extensive plans for the project, but he never travelled to Jerusalem and the only plan which survived eventually became *Madonna of the Lilies*.

The publisher Levy commissioned a follow-up volume to the highly successful *Documents Décoratifs*. Mucha began work on *Figures Décoratives*, but few would argue that it lacks the splendour of the first volume, that it undoubtedly suffered from his ongoing mood of despondency and apathy. At the age of forty-three, Mucha began to witness the death of many of his friends, including Colonel de Rochas, Brozik and Marold. Those friends who remained were intent on marrying him off, regarding him as an unfulfilled husband and father. Mucha studiously avoided their efforts, he had no intention of marrying whatsoever.

During this time, a twenty-one-year-old Czech student arrived in France. Maruska Chytilova had been invited by family friends to spend some time in Montmercy, close to Paris. This young woman was beautiful and unusually well-educated; she had studied art, she greatly admired literature and she was a Czech citizen. Mucha had always protested that if, one day, he was lunatic enough to marry, the lady in question would have to be a Czech. Maruska was keen to take advantage of Paris' many prestigious art académies. She enrolled at the Académie Julian for classes in drawing and painting. Her uncle was a prominent art historian at Prague University whom Mucha had met when he visited there. Maruska promptly wrote to him, expressing her wish to meet one of the Académie Julian's most famous pupils. She was not enjoying Paris. She had come full of enthusiasm and with the intention of visiting the Louvre, Nôtre-Dame and the many theatres in the city. Her hosts in Montmercy had other plans for her. She was expected to look after their children and was prohibited from visiting any of the sights of Paris unless accompanied by them. She had little time for drawing and had resigned herself to returning home disappointed when she received a reply from her uncle.

He had written her a letter of introduction to Mucha and instructed her to send it off to rue Val-de-Grâce. Mucha responded positively, as was his nature, to her request to call on him. The young art student could hardly believe that she would soon meet the great master and was filled with trepidation and fear. As soon as she arrived at his studio, Mucha put her at ease; he led Maruska to a large armchair and immediately began to question her about life in Czechoslovakia. They talked freely and she expressed her disappointment that she had seen nothing of Paris. Mucha agreed to remedy this situation. He invited Maruska to visit the theatre to see Sarah Bernhardt in her production of *Les Dames aux Camelias*. He also invited her to study with him for the remainder of her time in Paris and before long, she had found herself a room close to his studio in the city's Latin Quarter. In a letter home, she expressed her determination, like Mucha before her, to avoid all romantic relationships and to remain independent:

> *I continue going to Mucha of course; those are always the best moments in the whole week. Next week I'm going with him to the Bernhardt Theatre to see La Dame aux Camelias. I'm terribly excited ... He's good looking, even if he starts to show grey hair, but I won't fall in love with him. I admire him too much.*

Mucha saw Maruska regularly until she returned home a month later to Bohemia. By the time of her departure, they had fallen in love and Parisians had begun to gossip about the famous painter and his pretty, young student. In between writing long, regular letters to her, Mucha was now beginning to seriously question his future in Paris. A thought took root in his mind that he could easily make his fortune in America. Sarah Bernhardt had made millions there on her various theatrical tours, enough to finance those personal projects which satisfied her deeply, yet weren't necessarily commercial successes. Mucha had the same goal in mind. He was not travelling to the States to earn fame, but to earn money which was intended to finance *The Slav Epic*. Maruska had introduced another complication. How could he ever marry when he had nothing to show for all his years of popularity. He would travel to America, using Sarah's connections to ensure that he was successful in the art world there. She had already promised to help him in any way possible. Above all, Mucha needed an escape from Paris, an escape from his contractual obligations to Champenois and from the whole dying movement of *art nouveau*.

In 1904, Mucha was introduced to the Baroness Rothschild through an opera-singer friend, Boza Umirov. He confided in the Baroness his ambition to divorce himself from commercial art work and to travel to America to new pastures and a more lucrative career. Baroness Rothschild was keen to encourage the serious side of Mucha's work and suggested he should turn to portrait painting, like Sargent, who was currently taking on expensive commissions for wealthy Americans, with tremendous financial success. She immediately volunteered herself as an experimental model on whom Mucha could test his ability, and eventually commissioned a portrait of the

Ruby, from **The Four Jewels**.

A drawing entitled **Oriental Poppies** taken from *Documents Décoratifs,* **1902** (Cleveland Museum of Art). The importance of the floral motif cannot be overestimated when describing Mucha's work. He uses floral patterns generously and consistently to adorn the female form and to elevate women to god-like stature.

entire Rothschild family. Mucha set about completing all the commercial projects he had undertaken and he did not breathe a word about his imminent departure to anybody, not even to Maruska. He may well have feared that his publishers would come to hear of his decision and prevent him from leaving the city.

Art nouveau had run its course in Paris. One after another, its old adherents were abandoning the tenets of the movement and shifting their attentions to something less frivolous. The movement was remarkable for its brevity; it could not hope to survive the dramatic changes and new ideals of the twentieth century. Mucha had little difficulty abandoning it, simply because he had never felt himself part of *art nouveau*. His conscience was not troubled by any feeling of loyalty. He dropped a hint in a note to Maruska that he would be making a journey. She wrote a letter by return, demanding to know Mucha's destination. He wrote a hasty reply:

You ask about my journey. It's like this: I'm supposed to be well known in America, perhaps even more so than in Europe. People have been persuading me to go there, arguing that I might work there on more important things than here. Besides, from various quarters good offers have been made to me. So I've decided to go and have a look.

America eagerly awaited Mucha's arrival, the Press primed itself for his reception. Baroness Rothschild had already arranged Mucha's first portrait commission for him in New York. She provided him with letters of introduction to some of the wealthiest millionaire families, including the Vanderbilts and the Goulds and promised to join him there herself in due course. Mucha departed for America on 26 February, 1904. It was to be the first of many trips to the United States. He was in high spirits as he boarded the sailing vessel, *La Lorraine*, and could only think of the good things that were bound to follow. His words, written to Maruska the night before he left, proved strangely prophetic: '... immediately I have access into the highest American society. But better not count the chickens before they are hatched.'

CHAPTER 4

The American Dream

Seeds that had been
scattered during the
decades leading up
to the 1900s flowered
magnificently in their soil
to produce a New World
of possibility and
progress. America had
come into full bloom.

Overleaf:
Chocolat Masson, 1898 (Private collection). A detail from a popular calendar advertising one of Mucha's most important customers.

Opposite:
***Documents Décoratifs,* 1902** (Private collection). This detail shows all the characteristics of his style which Mucha hoped to pass on to both students and art enthusiasts. The drawings, either in colour or in black and white, were accompanied by his commentaries on his methods of achieving the finished piece.

As Europe faded into the distance, Mucha prepared himself to embrace this golden land of new beginnings. America had proven its love of the entrepreneur. It had nurtured promising children to safe adulthood, among them Rockefeller, Vanderbilt and Belmont and then carefully released them to the comforts of a millionaire lifestyle. America would hopefully extend this kindness to Mucha. He was keen to make an impression, eager to use his great gifts, unburdened by idealistic pursuits. He wanted to make money, and make it as quickly as possible. One thought was rooted firmly in his mind; it had not weakened since his departure from Paris. Why should he spend any more time on art which had cost him the best years of his life when he could earn as much as 5000 dollars for one single portrait? He would make a success of this venture and return to Europe with the resources necessary to begin work on his great historic masterpiece.

Before Mucha's arrival in America, there had been an upsurge of interest in *art nouveau*. The parallel American movement was greatly influenced by France, but it also had its own talented subscribers. Whistler first painted in the 'new style' as early as 1876, at a time when France was still immersed in classicism. Before he opened his exhibition of *art nouveau* in Paris, Bing had already visited the Chicago International Exhibition, where he managed to persuade three artists, Tiffany, Pennfield and Bradley to exhibit at his *Maison d'Art Nouveau* in Paris. The American journal, *The Chap Book*, whose style was exclusively *art nouveau*, had been appearing since 1894.

Mucha's famous reputation preceded him to New York. American society held him in such high regard that his arrival prompted extravagant coverage in the newspapers. The Sunday edition of the *New York Daily News* went so far as to devote both its front and back pages to Mucha. The feature contained colour reproductions of some of his *panneaux*, several pages of *Ilsée*, and a large portrait of him. Mucha described his reception in a letter to Maruska:

> *I went for a walk ... and a great surprise awaited me on the first street corner. Among the posters I saw my own life-size portrait – perfectly dreadful, needless to say – in crude colours on a red background ... There you are! The entire town was flooded with these things and, as I was told, also Philadelphia, Boston and other towns. The* New York Herald *also gave me a whole front page, as did* The Women's Journal *and other papers I have not yet seen but which are being sent to me.*

Mucha was again faced with a familiar problem, but he refused to acknowledge it. The American public expected him to continue to paint the *panneaux* and posters for which he had become famous in

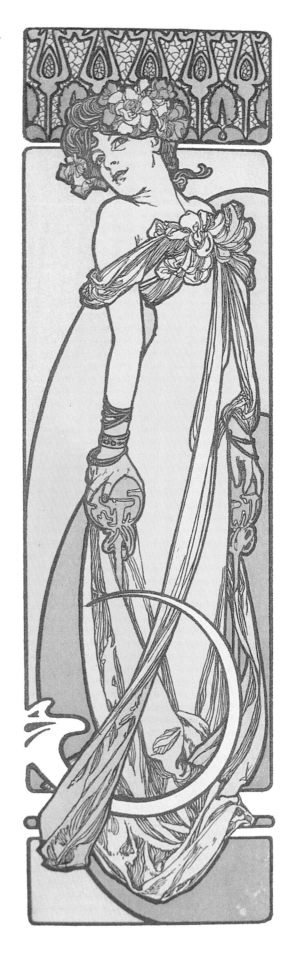

France. It came as a slightly unpleasant surprise to them when he stated his intention to paint portraits and to move on to more serious compositions. The newspapers had announced him as 'the world's greatest decorative artist', and he steadfastly set out to shrug off this tiresome image. He wanted to establish himself abroad as a serious painter and portraitist, to give himself a new identity. In an article in *The Sun* newspaper in April 1904, Mucha asserted:

> *It is four years now since I have done any* affiches *... They have had their day ... for it is a field which has been overworked, and while it served its purpose for a time I do not think of myself as a poster artist.*

Given that Mucha's motive for travelling to America was financial, it seemed a rather foolish move on his part to refuse commercial decorative work. His son Jiri has made a similar judgement:

> *Instead of using this opportunity which would have brought him the large sums of money he needed for his disinterested labours, he put the cart before the horse and began pig-headedly to deny his own past.*

The American élite readily invited Mucha to their homes. Lavish banquets were organized in his honour, various academic institutions showered him with accolades and degrees, prosperous ladies marvelled at his social grace and striking good looks. Whereas in Paris he had hated the notion of socializing on a grand scale, he was pleased to avail himself of the opportunity in America, perhaps realizing that it was a means to a lucrative end. Mucha's first portrait was of Mrs Wissman, a wealthy relative of Baroness Rothschild. He was accustomed to drawing portraits in pastels, but now, for the first time, he was obliged to adopt a whole new method and to paint his portraits in oil. Mucha admired American women for their very different beauty. In an article in *The World* he praised them over 'the anaemic type of Parisian beauty'. He found a strength and vigour in American females, they were at once 'svelte and solid'. Several more portrait commissions followed Mrs Wissman's, mostly of society women who found his charm irresistible. He painted Mrs Cornelius Vanderbilt, Elsie de Wolf, Mrs Morgan and the wealthy and beautiful Mrs Mackay.

Portrait painting proved to be a laborious, tedious task, however, both for the artist and the model. Mucha was rarely happy with what he had painted and he was not proficient enough with a brush to capture the desired image in one or two sittings. After twenty years of drawing with pencils, pastels and crayons, he found himself struggling with the detail and the proper blend of colour often difficult to

An example of the famous *panneaux*, elongated in shape and featuring, almost without exception, a single female form, transformed into a goddess. These drawings were reproduced in **Documents Décoratifs** in order to instruct his admirers (Private collection).

achieve in oils. He was bored also by the restrictions of naturalistic representation he assumed his portrait customers demanded. Although a master draughtsman, he often required ten, twenty or more sittings with the model to get the picture right. He invariably decided that his pictures needed re-touching. His knowledge of art served him little in his painting of portraits. Mucha could not appreciate the difference between drawing and painting, yet he maintained a cheerful trust in his own ability and convinced himself that it was a technique he would master in the fullness of time.

After only a couple of months in New York, Mucha realized that his plans to make his fortune were not going as smoothly as he had imagined. He was forced to compete with Sargent, the master painter of portraits, who delivered work of outstanding quality. The best of Mucha's paintings of this period are his portraits of children, such as *Rose of Sharon*, in which he was able to capture the spirit of the child, and focus to a much lesser degree on a perfect likeness. Both artistically and financially, he now found himself in a worse position than he had been in Paris. Because he was keen to pursue his notion of serious art to the bitter end, he would become involved in time-consuming projects from which he gained very little monetary reward. One such project, which occupied him for many years, yet brought him no money, was his portrait of New York's Archbishop Farley. As always, Mucha was anxious to form a social bond with his fellow-countrymen; he socialized with many Czechs in New York and also became involved with the Catholic church. The Catholic newspaper, *The New World*, was anxious to announce its affiliation with an artist of such stature:

> *Alphonse Maria Mucha ... was educated for the priesthood and so deeply did he imbibe the spirit of Catholic tradition and of Catholic theology, that they became the determining factors of his artistic career ... We fervently hope that Mucha can be induced to remain permanently in America ... Here beyond all question he could found the greatest school of religious art in the world; he would inculcate the grand principles of the Catholic tradition into the minds of thousands of pupils ...*

A prominent Catholic priest and friend of the Archbishop in New York by the name of Father Prout, set out to exploit Mucha's sentimental attachment to his religion and to the Czech nation. He persuaded Mucha, not only to paint the Archbishop's portrait, but to design several frescoes for the Convent of the Sacred Heart, by which he would be remembered abroad as a famous Czech artist, spreading his light to the American nation. Both enterprises were undertaken without a fee and they consumed a large amount of Mucha's time. He made detailed plans for the Madonna frescoes and spent many years on the

Chocolat Mexicain, 1898, and Chocolat Masson, 1898. This series of illustrations provides some later examples of Mucha's work for Champenois in the commercial field (Private collection).

Chocolat Mexicain

Chocolat Masson

1898

OCTOBRE	NOVEMBRE	DÉCEMBRE
1 s s Rémi, év.	1 m TOUSSAINT	1 j s Eloi
2 D ss Anges	2 m Les Morts	2 v ste Aurélie
3 l s Fauste	3 j s Hubert	3 s François X.
4 m s François d'A.	4 v s Charles B.	4 D ste Barbe
5 m ste Enimie	5 s s Théotime	5 l s Sabas
6 j s Arthur	6 D s Léonard DQ	6 m s Nicolas DQ
7 v s Serge DQ	7 l s Ernest	7 m s Ambroise
8 s ste Brigitte	8 m s Godfroy	8 j IMMAC. CONC.
9 D s Denis	9 m s Mathurin	9 v ste Léocadie
10 l s Florent	10 j s Juste	10 s ste Julie
11 m s Placide	11 v s Martin	11 D s Daniel
12 m s Wilfrid	12 s s René, év.	12 l ste Constance
13 j s Edouard	13 D s Brice	13 m ste Lucie NL
14 v s Calixte	14 l s Amand NL	14 m s Nicaise Q-T
15 s ste Thérèse NL	15 m ste Eugénie	15 j s Mesmin
16 D s Léopold	16 m s Edme	16 v ste Adélaïde
17 l ste Edwige	17 j s Agnan	17 s ste Yolande
18 m s Luc, évang.	18 v s Maxime	18 D s Gatien
19 m ste Laure	19 s ste Elisabeth	19 l s Timoléon
20 j s Aurélien	20 D s Edmond PQ	20 m ste Philog. PQ
21 v ste Ursule	21 l Prés. de la V.	21 m s Thomas ILv.
22 s s Modéran PQ	22 m ste Cécile	22 j s Honorat
23 D s Hilarion	23 m s Clément	23 v ste Victoire
24 l s Raphaël	24 j ste Flora	24 s ste Irmine v.j.
25 m s Crépin	25 v ste Catherine	25 D NOEL
26 m s Evariste	26 s ste Delphine	26 l s Etienne
27 j ste Antoinette	27 D AVENT	27 m s Jean, ap. PL
28 v s Alfred	28 l s Sosthène PL	28 m ss Innocents
29 s s Donat PL	29 m s Saturnin	29 j ste Eléonore
30 D s Arsène	30 m s André	30 v s Roger
31 l ste Lucille v.j.		31 s s Sylvestre

F. Champenois - Paris.

portrait of Archbishop Farley, transporting it back and forth across the Atlantic, yet never finishing it completely.

By May 1904, Mucha was on his way back home to Europe. After a brief spell in Paris, he journeyed to Bohemia and to Maruska. Although they made no formal announcement, everybody considered the couple to be engaged and it was understood that they should soon be married. Mucha journeyed from Bohemia to Jeand-Heures, where he spent the summer working on the painting *Madonna of the Lilies* and devoting whatever time he absolutely must to *Figures Décoratives*. He could hardly wait for Levy's tiresome commission to be completed so that he might get on with painting his own things. At the end of the summer, he returned to Paris with the intention of departing swiftly for America. Baroness Rothschild had also returned to Paris and had heard rumours of Mucha's imminent marriage to Maruska. She was furious and dismissed the notion of him marrying as foolish and detrimental to his artistic career. She withdrew her support and friendship, with the result that Mucha hesitated to return to the United States for a second visit.

During 1905, he eventually made a second and also a third trip. The first was in January, lasting six months, the second in November, lasting until the summer of 1906. He was now under far greater pressure to earn a respectable wage. Nevertheless, he continued to work on the projects for the Catholic church, while turning down other lucrative orders, including one from the millionaire Charles Schwab, to design a decorative panel for his entrance hall. The teaching job he accepted at the New York School of Applied Design for Women was at least one step in the right direction, but although Mucha enjoyed his position here, there was very little else on offer.

By January 1906, he had decided to compromise himself a little more and reverted to doing some of his old work. He was dreadfully crushed by his lack of success and resorted to drawing some illustrations for a fashion magazine called *Town Topics*. It was a humiliating exercise. He submitted the drawings, but could not admit that he had fallen so low. He announced to the editor that they had been produced by one of his students. At this time he also drew some designs for Armour, a Chicago firm of soap-makers. Although Mucha considered these drawings to be 'puny', the miniature panels, decorated with flowers and depicting elegant female forms in shades of violet, blue and green are reminiscent of some of his best early *panneaux*. Slowly, he began to recover from this low period. He received offers to lecture in Chicago and Philadelphia, he was asked to teach a new course at the New York Academy, and he was contacted by the Municipal Gallery in Philadelphia who wanted to exhibit his works to the American public. The exhibition opened in April 1906 and included such works as the *Madonna, Quo Vadis*, the originals of *The Lord's Prayer*, originals from

Chocolat Masson, 1898 (Private collection). Mucha made beautiful drawings for various calendars, filling every inch of the page with his trademark scrolls and flourishes.

Chocolat Mexicain (detail), 1898
(Private collection). The illustrations Mucha created for this calendar series are an example of his ability to enhance the commercial appeal of an everyday product by means of his splendid artistic gifts.

Documents Décoratifs and *Figures Décoratives*, together with various other drawings, sketches and portraits. Some eighty works in total were exhibited.

Mucha had decided that his wedding to Maruska should take place on 10 June in the little monasterial chapel of St Roche where he had slept for the first time as a young student before trying his luck at the Art Academy of Prague. He journeyed back to Europe for the third time and made his way to the Czech capital. By now, he had given up his studio in rue Val-de-Grâce and with some sadness, bid farewell to the city which had made him famous. The wedding was a festive event attended by all of Maruska's relatives. Mucha spent most of his honeymoon working on a new commission which he had accepted just before leaving New York. In his memoirs some years later, he described how looking at *The Seven Beatitudes* reminded him of the most beautiful time of his life.

When he returned to New York with his new wife, the majority of Mucha's time was given over to teaching, either at the New York Academy, or at the Art Institute of Chicago, or in Philadelphia. At the Institute of Chicago, he regularly lectured over five hundred pupils and never failed to stress the importance of a national art, untainted by foreign influences. He insisted that a nobility of character must be at the back of all great works of art, that conscientious, patient study of nature could alone enable the student to 'arrive', even in imaginative decoration. If the student would only draw from nature, then he would have nothing to unlearn. Nothing could be more fatal to the development of a great art than to copy the works made by another race. He pronounced the same opinions again and again: 'I can only teach the grammar, the technique, not the art; that must come from within and should be that expression of their national life.'

Maruska saw to it that Mucha kept a firm head on his shoulders. He was not so ready to refuse commissions which he considered 'beneath him' as he had been before. In the spring of 1908, he was visited by Dr Baumfeld, a representative of a committee of well-to-do Germans living in the United States. This group was keen to build a new luxury theatre in the centre of New York at the corner of Madison Avenue and Fifty-Ninth Street, and it wanted the interior decorated with dramatic hand-painted panels. Mucha was an obvious choice to complete this task and he very willingly accepted the commission. The project had to be completed within the space of only four months. Mucha enlisted the aid of one of his old students who had helped him work on the panels for the *Bosnian Pavilion* at the Great Exhibition of Paris. He rented a boathouse outside of the city and began to paint his last great work in the *art nouveau* style. He was desperately short of time, but the canvases, each measuring twelve feet by twenty-four feet, representing the birth of Beauty, Comedy and Tragedy, were the best

works he had managed to deliver to date during his stay in America. The designs met with the approval of the critics; many were astounded by Mucha's ability to maintain a tonal harmony in such vast compositions. Mucha found himself drawn into the world of theatre once again, keen to make his contribution, as he had done in Paris many years before.

Like so many other theatrical projects he became involved with during this time, the German Theatre proved to be a disastrous venture and its owners were obliged to close the building after only eight months. Mucha's next unsuccessful venture was a poster he designed for Leslie Carter. Carter's play *Kassa* opened in Washington in January 1909 and was an immediate failure. Mucha had thrown himself wholeheartedly into the production and it is doubtful whether he was ever paid for his work. In June of that same year, things began to improve slightly. A young actress named Maud Adams was due to appear as Schiller's *Maid of Orleans* at the Harvard University Stadium. Mucha drew the poster for this play, which was a notable success. He now had his foot in the door of the American theatre world and began to form valuable relationships. He painted a portrait of Ethel Barrymore, the star of *Lady Frederick*, a popular social figure, who liked to taunt the Press with her risqué love affairs and her endless string of engagements. He worked also on a number of extremely popular magazine covers, including *Hearst's, Colliers* and the *Ladies' Home Journal*, with renewed commercial success. He had not abandoned his dream of *The Slav Epic*, but it seemed no closer to fruition that it had been in Paris.

Mucha first met the millionaire Charles R. Crane at a banquet in 1904 – a political affair, organized as an unofficial demonstration against the Japanese-Russian war. Although they only met briefly, the two men seemed to understand each other and Mucha was immediately struck by Crane's ability to discuss the problems of the Slav people with intelligence and conviction. Crane was a regular visitor to the boathouse while Mucha worked there on the panels for the German Theatre. He was a remarkably silent man, calm, yet reassuring, passionately interested in world history and politics. He had earned his fortune in the plumbing industry and his philosophy of life was quite simple. He was not interested in money for its own sake, but only as a means to allow the individual to realize his more idealistic aims. He observed excitedly that the world was changing and he was keen to assist any movement which might accelerate this process. His money and power were important in strategic areas of socialist Europe. In 1905, he had built a vast factory in Petrograd and from here his influence had extended to the Far East and China.

Crane listened very attentively to Mucha's views on the Slavs in Europe and was impressed by this artist who wanted nothing more than to work for his country without any thought of profit. Mucha

discussed his main ambition with Crane – his desire to paint twenty vast panels in oil, depicting the little-known history of his native people from ancient times to the present. He explained to Crane the reasons for his exile from Europe and confessed that his desire to earn the necessary money for the project seemed to have gone disastrously wrong. Mucha was encouraged by Crane's response which, although noncommittal, could not readily be interpreted as an outright refusal. Crane immediately commissioned Mucha to paint his daughter's portrait. Mucha's painting of Josephine Crane Bradley symbolized the female figure of Slavia. It is now one of his best-known works, mainly because the portrait was printed on the first Czechoslovakian currency which appeared in 1918 and remained in circulation in the United States until the Second World War.

Crane had not yet made a final decision to finance *The Slav Epic*, but Mucha was optimistic that he would. He believed destiny would reveal the path forward sooner or later. He refused further commissions in America, resigned from his position at the Academy and announced to Maruska that they would soon be travelling back to Bohemia to begin work on his great epic. In 1910, Mucha left America and travelled to Czechoslovakia. Crane had finally sent him a positive reply and a cheque for 7500 dollars in support of his monumental project. Two immediate tasks awaited Mucha when he arrived back in Prague. He had agreed to decorate part of the Municipal Building and he was also faced with the problem of finding a studio which would house the vast canvases he intended to produce. He decorated the ceiling of the Municipal Building with the figure of a great eagle, its

An example of Mucha's more 'serious' art. The subject is still female, but Mucha now turns to oil painting and to a more naturalistic representation of form. The characteristics of *art nouveau* have all but disappeared. Colours are still muted, but the artist's clarity of outline suffers in this medium. Mucha was never as comfortable with a brush as he was with pencils or pastels (Collection HJERT).

wings outstretched. The impressive bird is encircled by an intricately patterned turquoise band, and an array of beautiful, ornamental figures form the border of the overall circular design.

The Czech public admired Mucha's work but, once again, Czech artists were incensed that Mucha should be asked to contribute to the art of a nation he had so freely abandoned in his youth. Mucha was deeply hurt to have his patriotism thrown back in his face, but he was also more determined than ever to present his ultimate gift to the nation.

The studio Mucha required to work on *The Slav Epic* was discovered quite by accident while visiting an old castle in Zbiroh with a close friend. One of the rooms they entered revealed a ray of sunshine streaming through a cracked pane of coloured glass in the roof. Mucha sent a man outside to break some more of the glass and the vast hall filled with light. This castle, hidden in the countryside, surrounded by forests and streams, perfectly served Mucha's needs. He began work on *The Slav Epic* in 1911, having already completed a good deal of his historical research. He had consulted every available volume on Czech history and had met with many of the most prominent historians from other Slav countries. He would fire his imagination from time to time by making tours of the Slav provinces. With sketchbook in hand, he would make pencil drawings of local peasants, or photograph them in traditional costumes. The work was painstaking and exhausting for an artist of his age, but he was motivated by the passion of a dream turning to reality before his eyes. He is known to have spent up to ten hours a day on an eighteen-foot scaffold platform, meticulously painting in the detail:

> *He used a technique which was probably based on his experience of scene painting with Brioschi-Kautsky in Vienna, and which he improved on as the work progressed. First he tried out the composition in a small sketch, working on it until he was satisfied with the arrangement of figures and space. Then he made a larger sketch, about 60 by 40 cm, for trying out the colours. Then he did a minutely detailed drawing of the same size in pen and water-colour. He now fixed strips of tracing paper on the prepared canvas, and by using a grid enlarged the whole picture from the sketch to its proper size. The entire drawing in charcoal on tracing paper was then taken down, perforated, and traced onto the canvas. Then, using the coloured sketch as a guide, the whole picture was undercoated with the principle colours. The drawing was traced on again, and he could now begin on the detail work. All the undercoating was done in egg tempera, and the details were finished in oils.*

His son's account offers some indication of the magnitude of Mucha's great, final work. Zbiroh castle, where Mucha worked on *The*

The Slav Epic, 1916. Mucha spent over twenty years on his series of historic paintings known as *The Slav Epic*. This oil canvas entitled *First Armed Meeting of the Hussites at Krizky (1419)* was painted in 1916 (Galerie de Hauptstadt, Prague).

Slav Epic, was Jiri Mucha's first home. He was born in 1915 when his father was fifty-five. In spite of the fact that there was little contact between them, Jiri remembers him as a warm old gentleman, a loving parent keen to encourage his son to paint and to draw. Jiri never mastered the art of drawing and painting but his father's instruction at least brought an appreciation of why his work was so difficult to copy. The first three pictures of *The Slav Epic* were completed quite quickly, by December 1912, but the impact of the six-by-eight-metre canvases is quite astounding. *Slavs in their Prehistoric Homeland* and *The Svantovit Festival* are two of the best known of the whole series of twenty. Like those to follow, they were conceived in a spirit of intense gratification. The pride Mucha felt in his native race comes through in every drawing. He was proud of Czech folk traditions, proud of the artistic culture of the Slav people. The project which was to occupy him for the next twenty years, is best described by Anna Dvorak in her book *Alphonse Mucha: Illustrations and Mural Paintings*:

> *The figural studies are faultless, there is none of the awkwardness of poses and problems with the space and with foreshortening that may be found in the works of more painterly painters. The combination of egg tempera and oil enabled the artist to adhere to his famous muted colouring and to accentuate it with more colourful details ... Mucha's greatest personal contribution is in the stylistic approach to both reality and allegory, to the story and its symbolic meaning, to man existing here and now ... The combination of history, painting and symbolism ... illustrates the development of the artist who reverted to his original interest, immeasurably enriched by his involvement with the decorative arts.*

Work on *The Slav Epic* was interrupted by yet another trip to the United States in 1913. During this time, Mucha finished all outstanding projects, including the portrait of Mrs Leatherbee, Charles R. Crane's second daughter. He then wound up his affairs and moved back to Europe permanently.

With the outbreak of the First World War in 1914, he handed his first three paintings to the Prague City Council for safe-keeping. Mucha feared for his own safety as well as for the safety of his art. After a number of visits from Austrian officials, he decided that the paintings on which he was still working should be made easy to remove from his studio. He devised a way of rolling up the huge canvases and placing them in metal tubes to be hidden in the depths of the forest. He worked on the Russian picture during this time, which had been inspired by a trip he made to Russia in 1913. The *Hussite Triptych* consists of a large central picture and two smaller wing panels which explore the history of the Czech Reformation.

The Slav Epic, 1916. Mucha set out to present to the public a world very close to his heart. His paintings are a dynamic representation of the most important moments in Slav history. Many of the figures depicted, often in traditional costume, are based on the sketches he made of folk cultures encountered first hand in the various Slav provinces to which he travelled (Galerie de Hauptstadt, Prague).

The Slav Epic was well received by a great deal of Mucha's admirers. The first eleven pictures were exhibited in the Carolinum Hall in Prague in 1919. The public loved his work because it reflected the sentiments of the people. Critics were less tolerant; one went so far as to describe the paintings as 'empty historic bombast'. The eleven pictures travelled to America and were exhibited at the Art Institute of Chicago with great success. In one week, fifty thousand people came to see Mucha's work. The next event was even more successful. An exhibition at the Brooklyn Museum opened in January 1921 and was visited by over 600,000 people, some of them declaring that *The Slav Epic* was the greatest work of the century.

In 1928, the paintings of *The Slav Epic* were eventually handed back to the city of Prague, which had always been Mucha's intention. He still could not satisfy himself that he had done enough for his country. He was busy designing new banknotes, postage stamps and even police-men's uniforms on a strictly voluntary basis. The State did not return his benevolence. Czech officials made little effort to find a permanent home for *The Slav Epic* and the paintings remained rolled up and housed in various storage facilities. The homelessness of his great work was a bitter pill for Mucha to swallow, yet he refused to criticize his nation.

Mucha continued working on *The Slav Epic* until the outbreak of the Second World War. In 1939, he was seventy-nine years old and quite frail. Czechoslovakia, his beloved country, had been invaded by the Germans, who immediately took him away for questioning. He did not survive the ordeal and died a few weeks later at his home. There can be no doubt that the German occupation of his homeland came as a terrible blow to Mucha. At the close of his life, he was made to witness an utter reversal of those dreams, proudly revealed at the end of the First World War, one still so familiar in his memory:

Today German oppression no longer weighs us down. We are free. But the mission of the Epic is not completed. Let it announce to foreign friends – and even to enemies – who we were, who we are, and what we hope for.

The Moravian Teacher's Choir, 1911 (Private collection), was one of Mucha's last posters evidently influenced by a Slavic theme. Mucha was in the process of working on *The Slav Epic* when this poster was produced. It depicts a Slav girl in folk costume, but has none of the brutal reality of his great series of oil paintings.

INDEX

Mucha. Bières de la Meuse, *c.* 1897
(Private collection)

Mucha. Cycles Perfecta, *c.* 1897
(Private collection)

Mucha. Salon des Cent, 1896
(Private collection)

Mucha. Poster for Job cigarette-papers
(Private collection)

Mucha. *Clio,* **1900**
(Private collection)

Mucha. The Four Flowers, 1897, Iris and **Carnation**
(Private collection)

Mucha. The Four Flowers, 1897, Lily and **Rose**
(Private collection)

Mucha. The Slav Epic, 1916
(Galerie de Hauptstadt, Prague)